PHOTOSYNTHESIS

ALVIN SILVERSTEIN • VIRGINIA SILVERSTEIN • LAURA SILVERSTEIN NUNN

TWENTY-FIRST CENTURY BOOKS

BROOKFIELD, CONNECTICUT

Cover photograph courtesy of ©Michael Hubrich, Science Source/Photo Researchers.

Photographs courtesy of Science Source/Photo Researchers: pp. 4 (© Kenneth Murray), 6 (© V. P. Weinland), 15 (© Hans Reinhard/Okapia), 16 © Science Photo Library), 20 (© Andrew Syred/SPL), 22 (© Dr. Kari Lounatmaa/SPL), 24 (© Microfield Scientific Ltd./SPL), 26 (© Geoff Tompkinson/SPL), 31 (© Lawrence Berkeley Laboratory/SPL), 33 (© Sylvain Grandadam), 37 (© Dr. Jeremy Burgess/SPL); Visuals Unlimited: pp. 10 (© Bud Nielsen), 11 (© Ken Lucas), 21 (© John D. Cunningham), 29 (© R. Howard Berg), 36 (© John D. Cunningham), 44, 47 (© D. Newman), 50 (© A. J. Copley), 52 (© Mark E. Gibson, inset © G. Chapman-P. Devadoss); Corbis-Bettmann: p. 14 (both); Animals, Animals: pp. 39 (Lynn M. Stone © 1994), 49 (© Patti Murray); AP/Wide World: p. 41.

Library of Congress Cataloging-in-Publication Data

Silverstein, Alvin.
Photosynthesis / Alvin and Virginia Silverstein and Laura Silverstein Nunn.
p.   cm. — (Science concepts)
Includes bibliographical references and index.
Summary: Explains photosynthesis, the process responsible for providing the material and energy for all living things, and discusses such related issues as respiration, the carbon cycle, acid rain, and the greenhouse effect.
ISBN 0-7613-3000-3 (lib. bdg.)
1. Photosynthesis—Juvenile literature. 2. Photosynthesis—Experiments—Juvenile literature.
[1. Photosynthesis.] I. Silverstein. Virginia B. II. Nunn, Laura Silverstein. III. Title.
IV. Series: Silverstein, Alvin. Science concepts.
QK882.S528   1998
572' .46—dc21   98-9279
                                                                              CIP
                                                                              AC

Published by Twenty-First Century Books
A Division of The Millbrook Press, Inc.
2 Old New Milford Road
Brookfield, Connecticut 06804

CONTENTS

ONE   **Food for Life**   5

TWO   **Milestones Along the Way**   12

THREE   **How It Works**   19

FOUR   **Photosynthesis Today**   34

FIVE   **Photosynthesis in the Future**   46

Glossary   55

For Further Information   59

Index   61

FOOD FOR LIFE

What is the most important process that takes place on earth? Many scientists would answer: **photosynthesis.** This process has made our planet livable for millions of living species. It also provides the materials and the energy that earth's creatures need to live and grow.

✦ FOOD FROM THE SUN ✦

All living things need energy in order to live. Most of the energy that living things on earth use comes from the sun. Sunlight is pure energy. But many of earth's creatures cannot use light energy directly. Green plants and a few other kinds of organisms can capture the energy in sunlight, and change it into chemical energy. This chemical energy is stored as food—energy-rich compounds that can be broken down later when energy is needed. Almost all other living things get their energy, either directly or indirectly, from the food made by plants.

Photosynthesis comes from two Greek words meaning "light" and "putting together." In photosynthesis, plants use sunlight energy to put together **carbon dioxide** from the air and water from the soil to make sugar.

During photosynthesis oxygen is given off as a by-product. Living things can use this oxygen "waste product" to get energy out of food. When a log burns in a fireplace, oxygen from the air combines with chemicals in the log, releasing their stored energy as heat. In a car engine, the burning of gasoline releases energy that is used to run the vehicle. In a similar way, oxygen is used in the bodies of living things to "burn" food for energy. Plants and other photosynthetic organisms supply all of the oxygen that is needed in our world.

Scientists believe that when the earth first formed, there was no oxygen in the air. Primitive plants and bacteria produced the first oxygen in our atmosphere by photosynthesis. Animals appeared later, when there was enough oxygen in the air to breathe.

Magic Trick

Plants are like magicians pulling a rabbit out of a hat—they make food out of thin air! Plants tap sunlight energy to make sugars out of carbon dioxide gas and water. The sugars are then used for energy, or when combined with minerals from the soil they are used as building materials to make plant tissues, proteins, fats, and all the other chemicals of life.

✦ GREEN POWER ✦

If photosynthesis is the most important biological process, then the substance that makes plants green, **chlorophyll**, could be considered the most important biological **molecule**. This colored chemical is found in many plant cells, particularly in the leaves, but also in the stems.

Chlorophyll is a **catalyst**. This means that it helps chemical reactions to take place, but the chlorophyll itself remains unchanged. When a particle of chlorophyll absorbs sunlight, a series of chemical reactions take place. Light energy is stored as chemical energy in handy "packets." The plant then uses the stored energy to run more chemical reactions, which produce sugar. Once the plant has formed sugar, it can make other, more complicated food substances, such as **cellulose**, **starches**, proteins, and fats.

Ferns are among the oldest kinds of land plants. They appeared 350 million years ago.

✦ SOLAR ENERGY ✦

The energy that reaches us from the sun is called electromagnetic radiation. Light is only a small part of the range, or spectrum, of electromagnetic radiation, which also includes X rays, microwaves, and gamma rays. Our eyes can see only visible light, the rainbow of colors from red to violet. Some animals, such as bees, can also see ultraviolet light (past the violet end of the rainbow). Heat-detecting goggles can pick up infrared light (past the red end of the light we can see).

Scientists argued for a long time about what light really is. It travels in waves, like the pattern of peaks and valleys on the surface of the ocean. But it also acts as if it is bundled into tiny particles, called **photons**. Each type of electromagnetic radiation has a different wavelength (the distance between peaks in the wave). The longer the wavelength, the smaller the amount of energy per photon. Red light has a longer wavelength than violet light; it contains only about half the energy per photon. Sunlight is a mixture of all the wavelengths of light energy, from the ultraviolet to the infrared.

✦ MAKING FOOD WITHOUT LIGHT ✦

In the 1970s scientists discovered communities of living organisms thriving on the deep ocean bottom, too far down for sunlight to reach. Huge red worms living in tubes, as well as new species of clams, crabs, jellyfish, and other ocean animals, were clustered around cracks, or vents, in the sea floor where molten lava had oozed out from the depths of the planet, producing currents of heated water rich in dissolved minerals. What were all these animals living on? There must be some food producers to support all these consumers, but how could they make food without a supply of sunlight energy?

Researchers found that the food producers in these ocean vent communities are bacteria that are very different from those living at the earth's surface. Instead of photosynthesis, they use a process called **chemosynthesis** to store energy in a special compound and convert carbon dioxide to biochemicals used for food and building materials. Scientists classify these bacteria as **lithotrophs** ("rock-eaters") because they get energy by oxidizing minerals such as sulfates, nitrites, and iron compounds, as well as chemicals such as hydrogen sulfide and ammonia. These are chemicals that were plentiful on the ancient earth, before photosynthesizers generated oxygen for the atmosphere.

Researchers believe that the bacteria that live by chemosynthesis are very ancient—perhaps the first living creatures that appeared on our planet. They have named them Archaebacteria, or Archaea, from the Greek word for "ancient."

In 1996 a team of British and Russian scientists working in the southern Ural mountains discovered the fossils of a seafloor vent community that thrived during the earth's Silurian period—438 million to 410 million years ago. The fossils included large tubeworms similar to those found at modern undersea vents.

ANCIENT WISDOM

The Old Testament says "all flesh is grass"—which reflects how, with a few exceptions, life on earth is possible because of the ability of green plants to capture the sun's energy.

✦ THE WEB OF LIFE ✦

Living things are linked together in an intricate web of life. This web of life is also a **food web**, for it is made up of many **food chains**. Each kind of organism in a food chain uses the next type in the chain as part of its food supply.

Living things are either **producers** or **consumers**. Producers produce food. Consumers cannot make their own food but must consume the food made by producers. If all living things were consumers, life on earth would cease when the food was all used up.

Producers make up the largest share of the **biomass**—the amount of living materials—on our planet. Producers are the living creatures that take energy from the sun to make food (first in the form of sugar) through photosynthesis. These sugar makers include green plants, algae, plankton, and photosynthetic bacteria.

WHAT DO PLANTS NEED?

Plant a corn seedling in each of four pots, each containing the same amount of soil.

- Place the first pot in the light, but do not water it.
- Water the second pot every day but keep it in a dark closet.
- Place the third pot in the light with a small cup of soda lime next to it. Water the pot and cover both the pot and the cup with a large-mouth jar. (Soda lime takes carbon dioxide out of the air. The pot needs to be watered only at the beginning of the experiment because the jar keeps the water from evaporating.)
- Place the fourth pot in the light and water it regularly.
- Compare the four plants after two weeks.

Primary consumers, or **herbivores**, get their sugar by eating plants. Herbivores include animals such as cows, deer, rabbits, mice, fruit- and seed-eating birds, most insects, and the plankton eaters of the oceans.

Animals (and some plants) that feed on plant-eating animals are secondary consumers, or **carnivores**. Carnivores include all of the members of the cat and dog family, most mammals that live in the sea, most reptiles, spiders, starfish, and even some plants, such as the Venus's-flytrap.

Some animals are both primary and secondary consumers. Bears, for example, eat fish and berries. Animals that eat a mixed diet are called **omnivores**. Humans are omnivores, too.

THINK ABOUT IT

Is it easier for plants to live without animals, or for animals to live without plants?

Bears prefer meat but vary their diet with fish, berries, ants, grubs, and the leaves and roots of some plants.

Dung beetles roll dung into balls, then lay their eggs in them. Their larvae feed on the dung. In this way, the beetles break down a waste product.

Even at the microscopic level, organisms that can't use the sun's energy are dependent on those that can. A photosynthetic bacterium, for example, is lunch for an amoeba.

Decomposers play an important role by breaking down the waste products and the dead bodies of the living creatures of all of the other three groups. Decomposers include bacteria, fungi, and some animals such as earthworms, dung beetles, and maggots.

MILESTONES ALONG THE WAY

Plants have played an important part in human history. The earliest humans hunted for meat but also gathered plant fruits, roots, and leaves to eat. They learned about what plants were good to eat and observed how plants grow. Eventually they got the idea of saving some of the seeds from good food plants to grow crops the next year. People first began to grow plants for food about 10,000 years ago. This new practice changed the way early humans lived. Before this time, people had to roam from place to place to find food. Now they could settle down and build permanent homes.

✦ ANCIENT IDEAS ABOUT PLANTS ✦

Aristotle and other ancient Greeks knew that the life processes of animals depended on the food they ate. But how did plants get *their* food? The soil was the only thing that people could see touching the plant's roots. So the ancient Greeks decided that plants must get all of their food from the soil. (Air touches plants too, but people can't see or feel air.) No one came up with a better idea until about 350 years ago.

✦ A CAREFULLY PLANNED EXPERIMENT ✦

A seventeenth-century Belgian physician named Jan Baptista van Helmont decided to find out for himself where plants really get the food they need to grow. First he weighed a wooden tub filled with dry soil. Then he weighed a willow shoot and planted the willow in the tub. For five years van Helmont added nothing but pure water to the tub. By then the willow shoot had become a small tree.

Van Helmont removed the tree and its roots, and dried the soil in the tub. The tree had gained about 165 pounds (75 kg) in weight, but the soil weighed only about 2 ounces (60 grams) less than it had when he started five years earlier. Obviously the tree did not get all of the materials it needed to grow from the soil, as people had thought for the previous 2,000 years! But van Helmont did not guess the real answer. Instead, he mistakenly concluded that the material that made up the bark, wood, roots, and leaves came from the water he had added over the five years.

✦ A CLOSER LOOK AT "AIR" ✦

The next important step in the understanding of photosynthesis occurred in the early 1770s. Joseph Priestley, the British scientist who is credited with discovering oxygen, knew that burning a candle in a closed container used up something in the air so that the flame would eventually go out. He found that a living sprig of mint helped to "restore" the air in a chamber so that a candle could burn again. He concluded that plants helped to "cleanse and purify our atmosphere." Priestley's experiment did not work when he moved the chamber to a dark corner of the laboratory, but he did not realize the importance of light in the process. (The mint sprig needed light to keep producing oxygen, which the burning candle used to produce a flame.)

After Priestley's discovery, hospitals began putting lots of flowers in sickrooms to "cleanse" the air. A Dutch physician, Jan Ingenhousz, wanted to find out whether flowers really could help cure illnesses. In 1779, after many different tests, he determined that only the green parts of plants "cleaned" the air—and only when placed in strong light. Flowers and other nongreen parts of the plant used up oxygen just like animals do!

In 1796 Ingenhousz suggested that this process of photosynthesis causes carbon dioxide to be split into carbon and oxygen. Then the oxygen is released as a gas.

Later, other scientists found that sugars contain carbon, hydrogen, and oxygen atoms in a ratio of one carbon molecule for each molecule of water (CH_2O). This is where the word **carbohydrate** comes from—*carbo*- for "carbon" and *hydrate* for "water." (Carbohydrates are a family of chemical com-

*Joseph Priestley (inset) and a drawing of his laboratory.
Priestley (1732–1804) published his discovery of oxygen in 1775
and moved from England to Pennsylvania in 1794.*

pounds including sugars and also starches, which are made up of large numbers of sugar units linked together.)

In 1804 Swiss scientist Nicholas Theodore de Saussure repeated van Helmont's experiment but carefully measured the amounts of carbon dioxide and water that were given to the plant. He showed that the carbon of plants comes from carbon dioxide and the hydrogen from water.

Forty years later, a German scientist, Julius Mayer, showed that the energy of sunlight is captured in photosynthesis.

✦ GREEN MAGIC ✦

Scientists wondered what it was that allowed plants to make their own food while animals cannot. Was it their green color? Other living things that are similar to plants but are not green, such as mushrooms, do not photosynthesize. Even green plants photosynthesize only in the parts that are green. A tree does not photosynthesize in its roots, bark, or branches.

Leaves come in many sizes and shapes,
but all green leaves produce chlorophyll.

Richard Willstatter
(1872-1941)

Two French scientists, Pierre Joseph Pelletier and Joseph Bienaime Caventou, isolated the green substance from plants in 1817 and named it chlorophyll, from Greek words meaning "green leaf." In 1883 Julius von Sachs showed that chlorophyll is not scattered all around a plant cell but is found in special structures called chloroplasts.

Chlorophyll is a complicated molecule, and it was not until 1906 that scientists began to understand more about it. German scientist Richard Willstatter found that there are two kinds of chlorophyll. One, which he named chlorophyll a, makes up three fourths of the chlorophyll in plants; the other, which he called chlorophyll b, accounts for the other one fourth. Willstatter found that chlorophyll contained carbon, hydrogen, oxygen, and nitrogen atoms, which was not surprising. But it also contained a metal, magnesium. This was the first molecule from a living thing to be found to contain magnesium.

Willstatter received a Nobel Prize in chemistry in 1915 for his work on chlorophyll. In 1965 an American scientist, Robert Burns Woodward, won a Nobel Prize in chemistry for figuring out the structure of the chlorophyll molecule.

✦ WHERE DOES THE OXYGEN COME FROM? ✦

The overall reaction for photosynthesis was thought to be

$$CO_2 + H_2O + \text{light energy} \rightarrow (CH_2O) + O_2.$$

carbon   water   carbohydrate   oxygen
dioxide

For many years scientists believed that the oxygen released came from the carbon dioxide molecule. Most accepted this idea until the 1930s, when a graduate student at Stanford University, C. B. van Niel, questioned it.

Van Niel was investigating the photosynthesis that occurred in different groups of bacteria, such as the **purple sulfur bacteria**. Purple sulfur bacteria create carbohydrates, but they do not release oxygen. Van Niel proposed that it was not carbon dioxide that is broken up to produce oxygen gas during photosynthesis, but the water molecule.

Later, investigators used special radioactive isotopes of oxygen to show that the oxygen that is released does indeed come from the water and not the carbon dioxide. So the proper equation for photosynthesis in algae and green plants is

$$6\ CO_2\ +\ 12\ H_2O\ \rightarrow\ C_6H_{12}O_6\ +\ 6\ O_2\ +\ 6\ H_2O.$$

carbon　　water　　　　　glucose　　　oxygen　　　water
dioxide　　　　　　　　　(a sugar)

Notice that water appears on *both* sides of this equation, and the total numbers of carbon, hydrogen, and oxygen atoms on the left side are equal to the corresponding sums on the right.

✦ THE LIGHT AND DARK SIDES OF PHOTOSYNTHESIS ✦

Photosynthesis is really a two-stage process—and light is necessary for only one of them! An English plant physiologist, F. F. Blackman, was the first to discover this. He reported in 1905 that one set of reactions is dependent on light and the other on temperature. The two stages are often called the "**light reactions**" and "**dark reactions**" of photosynthesis. The dark reactions use the products of the light reactions. Their names seem to imply that the light reactions occur only in the light and the dark reactions occur only in darkness. Actually, however, *both* sets of reactions take place in the light, but when a plant is in darkness the light reactions stop, and only the dark reactions continue. Light is not directly involved in the dark reactions.

Blackman found that the dark reactions go faster when the temperature is increased up to 30°C, but they slow down at higher temperatures. He concluded that these reactions are controlled by enzymes—special proteins that help reactions to take place. This has been shown to be true.

In the light reactions, light energy is used to form a special compound called **ATP** (adenosine triphosphate), whose chemical bonds can store energy and release it readily when it is needed. In the dark reactions, ATP is used to build simple sugars from carbon dioxide. The chemical energy of the ATP molecule is transferred to the bonds that hold the sugar molecule together. ATP itself loses one of its three phosphate units in the process and is converted to ADP (adenosine *di*phosphate).

In the 1940s at the University of California, Berkeley, a young scientist named Melvin Calvin conducted a series of experiments that worked out the complicated steps in which sugars are formed. Calvin grew algae in a glass chamber shaped like a big lollipop. He bubbled radioactively labeled carbon dioxide through the suspension in the green "lollipop" so that he could follow what happened to the specially tagged carbon atoms during the reactions of photosynthesis. At various times he dumped part of the mixture from the lollipop into a flask of boiling alcohol. That stopped the reactions immediately, and Calvin analyzed the sample to see which compounds in the mixture contained radioactive carbon. Each successive sample gave him an idea of what was going on at later and later stages in the process. Today the light-independent, or dark, reactions of photosynthesis are called the **Calvin cycle**, and the scientist won a Nobel Prize for his work.

THREE

How It Works

Plants are like busy factories. The main production areas are the leaves, where most of the work of photosynthesis is done. But the plant "factory" also includes supply lines to bring in raw materials and transport them to the work areas, energy-producing "furnaces" to power the work, storage areas for the finished products, and ways to get rid of waste products.

✦ ROOTS: ABSORPTION OF WATER AND MINERALS ✦

Soil contains water and minerals that plants need to grow. Minerals in the soil dissolve in water, just as salt dissolves when you pour it into a cup of water. Plant roots are anchored in the soil and absorb water with its dissolved minerals.

Tiny root hairs grow out from the tips of a root. There are billions of root hairs on most plant roots. The root hairs absorb most of the water that plants take in. The more root hairs, the greater the surface area available to absorb water.

✦ STEMS: TRANSPORTATION OF MATERIALS ✦

Water and minerals travel from the roots up to the leaves through the plant stem. A stem contains two types of tubes for transporting materials. Tubes called **xylem** bring water and minerals from the roots to the leaves. **Phloem** tubes carry food from the leaves to all parts of the plant.

This scanning electron micrograph shows a root covered with tiny water-absorbing root hairs.

✦ LEAVES: NATURE'S FOOD FACTORIES ✦

Leaves are usually flat and wide. This gives them a large surface in order for them to absorb as much sunlight as possible. The more leaves a plant has, the more sunlight it can absorb. A full-grown maple tree has about 100,000 leaves, with a total surface area of 2,000 square yards.

Leaves are made up of many parts. The top and bottom layers protect the insides of the leaf, the way a roof and floor protect a house. The top layer is clear, like a sunroof, to let in the sunshine. Beneath the outer layer is a layer of food-making cells. In another, a spongy layer of cells, food is stored before it is taken to the rest of the plant. The parts of the leaf are connected to the stem by veins.

A LOOK AT XYLEM TUBES

Put ten drops of red food coloring into a half cup of water. Cut off the bottom of a celery stalk and place it in the colored water. Let it sit overnight, then cut the celery in half to look at a cross section.

✦ STOMATES: THE GATEWAYS FOR GASES ✦

Carbon dioxide passes into plant leaves through tiny holes on the undersides of the leaves. Each of these special holes, called **stomates**, is surrounded by a pair of guard cells. When the guard cells are opened wide, gases can pass in and out of the stomates. When they are squeezed together, gases cannot enter or leave.

FIND THE STOMATES

Keep a geranium plant in a dark closet for three days. Then set the plant on a sunny windowsill. Put petroleum jelly on the top of one of the leaves and on the bottom of a different leaf. (The petroleum jelly will block up the stomates so that the leaf cannot "breathe.") Observe the geranium plant's leaves each day over the next week. (Remember to water the plant when the soil gets dry.) Compare the petroleum-coated leaves with one of the leaves that was not coated on either side. Can you tell which surface of the leaf contains the stomates?

Stomates (circles) surrounded by guard cells. Stomates are usually open when a leaf is making food. Guard cells control how much water vapor and carbon dioxide pass through stomates.

The food-making parts of plants contain chlorophyll, which makes the layer of food-making cells look green. Chlorophyll is found in parts of the cell called **chloroplasts**. Chloroplasts are energy-capturing **organelles**. (An organelle is a tiny working structure found in an individual cell). They are both solar cells and sugar factories. They capture the energy from sunlight, and they help produce plant food—sugar.

FIND THE CHLOROPHYLL

Ask an adult to help you with this activity. Observe and draw the pattern of colors of a coleus leaf. (The leaves of a coleus typically have varied patterns of green, white, and purple patches.) Carefully, wearing an oven mitt, boil the leaf in water for five minutes. Carefully remove the leaf from the hot water with a spoon. Then put the leaf into hot alcohol until the color has disappeared. Next, wearing gloves and an apron, put two drops of iodine on the leaf. Then rinse the leaf off in water. Compare the leaf to your drawing. (Iodine tests for starch.)

1. What happened to the leaf when you added iodine?
2. How can you tell where the chlorophyll was in the leaf?

The yellow lines in this enlarged view of chloroplasts are grana, which contain chlorophyll pigments.

Each chloroplast is made up of a smooth outer and inner membrane that enclose a chamber called the **stroma**. The stroma is filled with a thick, watery solution. Within the inner membrane is a third membrane that forms a complicated system of stacked disklike sacs, called **thylakoids**. These flattened sacs are interconnected by flattened channels. Each thylakoid has a space inside it, which is surrounded by the thylakoid membrane.

Each leaf cell contains about 50 or more chloroplasts. In a square millimeter of a corn leaf there can be 500,000 chloroplasts. The chloroplasts in all of the leaves of a full-grown maple or elm tree have a surface area of about

140 square miles (360 square km)! A single maple tree can produce 2 tons of food (sugar) on a sunny day.

CHLOROPHYLL WITHOUT CHLOROPLASTS

Blue-green bacteria are microscopic organisms. Some grow as single cells, some are masses of thin threads, and some form huge colonies. They contain chlorophyll, but they do not contain chloroplasts. Chlorophyll is spread throughout the cell. Many scientists believe that the chloroplasts in plant cells evolved from photosynthesizing bacteria much like these.

✦ PIGMENTS AND LIGHT ENERGY ✦

A pigment is any substance that absorbs light. If a pigment absorbs all wavelengths of light, it looks black. Some pigments absorb only certain wavelengths of light. The rest are reflected. Chlorophyll is a pigment that absorbs violet, blue, and red wavelengths. It reflects green wavelengths and so it looks green to us. Other plant pigments involved in photosynthesis include **carotenoids** (red, orange, and yellow pigments) and **phycobilins** (red and blue pigments).

When pigments absorb light, some of their **electrons** gain more energy. The "excited" electrons may then give off energy as heat or light. Or the energy may be captured in a chemical bond. This is what happens in photosynthesis.

✦ THE CHLOROPHYLL FACTORY ✦

Chlorophyll and other pigments, along with some special proteins needed for photosynthesis to occur, are embedded in the thylakoid membranes. Chlorophyll molecules are organized into groups of 250 to 400 pigment molecules. Each group is called a **photosystem**. Scientists believe that two kinds of photosystems work together to produce stored energy.

All of the pigment molecules in a photosystem can absorb packets of light energy called photons. But only one chlorophyll molecule in each photosystem can use light energy for **photochemical reactions**. This special chlorophyll molecule is called the photosystem's **reaction center**. The other pigment molecules are called **antenna pigments**, because they gather light energy like a network of antennas. The antenna pigments pass the light energy they have collected along to the reaction center, which gives its high-energy electrons to a neighboring molecule (an electron acceptor).

Chlorophyll can convert light energy to chemical energy only in the thylakoid membranes, working with their special proteins. When light shines on chlorophyll molecules in a test tube, the pigment molecules just absorb energy temporarily and then release it as heat and light, without performing any useful work.

TREMENDOUS LIGHT ABSORBERS

Chlorophyll molecules can absorb an enormous amount of light. Almost all of the red and blue light passing through a container of water will be absorbed if only a few milligrams of chlorophyll are placed in it.

A micrograph of a diatom showing pores and grooves of its cell wall. Diatoms form a large part of microscopic plankton.

There are several kinds of chlorophyll, which have somewhat different molecular structures. The blue-green chlorophyll a is the most common and is found in nearly all photosynthetic organisms. Many also contain the yellow-green chlorophyll b, as well. These two forms absorb light of different wavelengths. A plant that contains both can use more of the energy found in light. Only chlorophyll a molecules can transform light energy into a chemical bond, however. When light excites a chlorophyll b molecule, the molecule must transfer the energy to a chlorophyll a molecule in order for it to be used.

Some types of algae, such as brown algae and diatoms, have a different form, chlorophyll c, instead of chlorophyll b. Bacteria that do not produce oxygen as a waste product contain **bacteriochlorophyll** (in purple bacteria) or **chlorobium chlorophyll** (in green sulfur bacteria).

✦ HOW CHLOROPLASTS MAKE SUGAR ✦

Photons (packets of light energy) hit the chlorophyll molecules in leaves. Electrons are knocked into a higher-energy state. The electrons bounce along a series of chlorophyll and enzyme molecules and eventually reach small special carrier molecules in the thylakoid membrane. The electrons create a current as they flow down along this **electron transport chain**, and some of their energy is used to form an ATP molecule.

Meanwhile, the missing chlorophyll electrons have to be replaced, or else the chlorophyll molecules can no longer be used. They are replaced by electrons from water molecules, so that the chlorophyll molecule is ready for action once again. (A special enzyme splits water molecules—H_2O—into two electrons, two hydrogen ions, and one oxygen atom.)

High-energy electrons and hydrogen ions combine with a substance called **NADP** (nicotinamide adenine dinucleotide phosphate) to form NADPH, which then supplies energy to the food-making reactions of photosynthesis.

So far we have described the "light reactions," which must take place in sunlight. They occur in the thylakoid or photosynthetic membranes. They are followed by the "dark," or "light-independent reactions," of photosynthesis, which produce sugars. These dark reactions take place in a different part of the chloroplast: the stroma, the space outside of the thylakoid sac.

A team of enzymes helps finish the sugar-making process through a series of chemical reactions. Using ATP molecules for energy, carbon dioxide from the air is combined with the "hot" hydrogens on NADPH, eventually producing sugar after a series of enzyme reactions. The energy that was stored in the chemical bonds of the high-energy carriers ATP and NADPH is released and stored in the bonds of sugar molecules.

✦ LIFE'S BUILDING BLOCK ✦

Glucose is a simple sugar, whose molecule contains six carbon atoms combined with twelve hydrogen atoms and six oxygen atoms. It is the basic building block for the other materials that make up living things. Glucose molecules are put together to form large molecules of starch, for food storage. Cellulose is a struc-

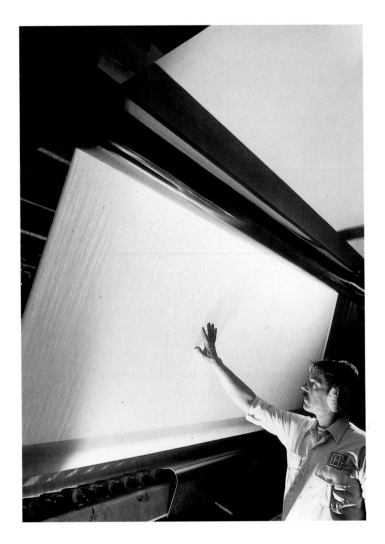

Much of the paper manufactured today is made from wood pulp, which is composed mainly of cellulose.

tural material made from even larger numbers of glucose units. Cellulose forms the outer walls of plant cells and is the main substance found in wood. Paper and cotton are nearly pure cellulose. Glucose can be converted to fats and oils, which are more concentrated energy reserves than sugars and starches. Minerals that are absorbed from the soil are combined with glucose molecules to form other, more complicated biochemicals. Glucose can be converted to amino acids, which form the many thousands of kinds of proteins that are found in living things. Glucose can also be converted to nucleotides, the building blocks of RNA and DNA, the chemicals of heredity.

WHAT HAPPENED TO THE DINOSAURS?

If there is no photosynthesis occurring, there is no food produced. One theory about why the dinosaurs disappeared suggests that a massive comet or meteor hit the earth with such force that huge clouds of dirt, dust, and other particles rose up from the ground into the atmosphere, blocking out the sunlight for a long time. (Other scientists think a large volcano spewed out thick clouds of material, with the same effect.) Without sunlight, many plants would have died, and the dinosaurs that depended on them would have died, too.

✦ CARBON DIOXIDE TRAPS ✦

Plants get carbon dioxide from the air. Special sugarlike molecules found in the plants act as carbon dioxide traps to hold tightly onto the carbon dioxide molecules that are absorbed from the air. Six trapped carbon dioxide molecules are needed to make one molecule of the simple sugar glucose.

If plants need sugarlike carbon dioxide traps in order to make sugars by photosynthesis, how do these molecules get to be in the plant tissues in the first place? Young plants make the biochemicals they need using the stored building blocks and energy provided by their parents.

Most green plants form seeds or spores in order to produce a new generation of green plants. Seeds contain a supply of starch or other food for the plant to use for energy when it is first starting out. The energy stored in the seed is used to build the roots and green shoot that grows above the ground, and also to make chlorophyll, carbon dioxide traps, and the other compounds needed for photosynthesis. By the time the stored food supply is all used up, the plant is ready for photosynthesis to take over.

✦ LIFE DEPENDS ON A WASTE PRODUCT! ✦

When water molecules are split into hydrogen and oxygen during photosynthesis, the hydrogen combines with carbon dioxide to form glucose molecules. Some of the oxygen is used by the plant, but the rest is released into the air. The waste product of photosynthesis in plants—oxygen—is a substance nearly all of the earth's creatures cannot live without.

ANOTHER SOURCE OF ELECTRONS

Oxygen is produced as a by-product of photosynthesis because plants need a source of electrons to replace those that are used in photosynthesis. But water doesn't have to be the source of the electrons. Some photosynthetic organisms, such as sulfur bacteria, use different compounds.

Sulfur bacteria are found in underwater sulfur springs or in volcanoes where a lot of hydrogen sulfide is found. These bacteria use hydrogen sulfide as their source of electrons. Instead of producing oxygen as a by-product, they produce large amounts of pure sulfur when they grow.

It's a good thing that bacteria that produce oxygen evolved, or else we wouldn't be here!

Why do animals need oxygen? Plants form food products using sunlight and carbon dioxide from the air. Oxygen allows animals to use the energy trapped inside this food. The oxygen that animals breathe in is used to "burn" the food to release the trapped energy. In a process called **respiration**, energy is released from the food materials, and carbon dioxide and water are given off. The process of respiration is the opposite of the process of photosynthesis.

Two kinds of tiny organelles are responsible for the way living things handle the energy that flows through life. Chloroplasts use the energy of light to build sugar through photosynthesis. **Mitochondria** break down sugar in both plant and animal cells. In this process of respiration, ATP is produced. When the

*An enlarged view
of mitochondria in
a plant cell*

ATP is used by the cell, heat is released, as the last stage of the flow of energy. The flow of energy through life can thus be described as:

$$\text{sunlight} \rightarrow \text{sugar} \rightarrow \text{ATP} \rightarrow \text{heat.}$$

Chloroplasts and mitochondria are similar in many ways. Both organelles are elongated and about the size of bacteria. Both carry out energy-related tasks. The two phases of respiration take place in areas that are similar to those in which the two stages of photosynthesis occur in chloroplasts. Both organelles contain their own genetic material. Both have a complex membrane. Mitochondria are powerhouses that produce ATP, but chloroplasts are a combination solar cell and sugar factory.

PHOTOSYNTHESIS vs.	RESPIRATION
Needs sunlight	Does not need sunlight
Occurs in cells with chlorophyll	Occurs in all living cells
Uses water	Gives off water
Uses carbon dioxide	Gives off carbon dioxide
Gets energy from sun	Releases energy from sugar
Makes sugar	Breaks down sugar
Gives off oxygen	Uses oxygen

The sugar-producing reactions that Melvin Calvin and his coworkers discovered involve nearly two dozen enzymes in a complex series of steps. The most important is the first step, in which CO_2 is linked to a five-carbon sugar called **RuBP** to form a six-carbon sugar. The newly formed sugar quickly breaks up into two three-carbon compounds. These are the first stable products in the production of carbohydrates. For this reason the pathway to producing carbohydrates is often called the C_3 cycle.

EARTH'S NO. 1 PROTEIN

The enzyme involved in joining CO_2 and the five-carbon sugar in the first step of the Calvin cycle is a special protein called **rubisco**. There is more of this protein in the world than any of the millions of other proteins found in living things on our planet!

The first three-carbon compound formed in the Calvin cycle, called **3-PGA**, is changed into an energy-rich three-carbon sugar, G3P, in reactions using the energy stored in ATP and electrons from NADPH. Two molecules of G3P then combine to form the six-carbon sugar **glucose**.

Oddly enough, though, it takes six full turns through the reactions of the Calvin cycle to produce just one glucose molecule. For every six G3P's that are produced in one turn of the carbon cycle, only one moves on through steps that will create glucose and other carbohydrates. The rest pass through the Calvin cycle again to produce more RuBP and keep the process turning. The three-carbon sugars must go through a number of steps forming five-, six-, and seven-carbon sugars before RuBP is produced. They use up ATP in this process. It may seem inefficient, but the reactions occur quickly and there is plenty of RuBP to keep the process going smoothly.

Scientists call the process of taking the carbon atom from CO_2 and using it in organic materials "fixation." They say that ATP and NADPH provide the chemical energy to "fix" CO_2 to produce carbohydrates.

Glucose, the six-carbon sugar that is produced through photosynthesis, can be used in a number of ways. It may be stored in the chloroplast itself as starch granules. It may be converted into lipids and oils, which are also stored in the

*In the 1950s Melvin Calvin determined
the chemical process of photosynthesis.
He won the Nobel Prize for chemistry in 1961.*

chloroplast. Or it may be transported out of the chloroplasts to be used by the rest of the plant cell.

✦ DOING IT THEIR WAY ✦

Calvin and his associates learned about photosynthesis by studying green algae, but the cycle of reactions they discovered is very common in the plant world, too. **C_3 plants** are found all over the world and include important food crops such as wheat, rice, soybeans, and oats. But not long after the Calvin team discovered the C_3 pathway, two Australian scientists found that some plants use a different pathway to incorporate carbon dioxide into organic materials. The first stable product produced in this photosynthetic pathway is a four-carbon compound sugar instead of the three-carbon one produced in other plants. This has become known as the C_4 pathway, and it is common among plants that have adapted to grow in conditions of low moisture and bright sunlight. There are more than one hundred genera of **C_4 plants**, including corn, sugarcane, and Bermuda crabgrass.

When the climate is very dry and the sun is brightly shining, most plants take measures to conserve water. They close the stomates on the undersides of the leaves to cut down the loss of water into the air. But then CO_2 cannot get into the leaf through the closed stomates. The amount of carbon dioxide inside the leaves drops, and oxygen builds up. The C_3 plant switches from photosynthesis to a different process, called **photorespiration**, which uses O_2 and produces CO_2 and water but no sugars. C_4 plants have an advantage under these conditions. They can continue the process of photosynthesis at much lower concentrations of CO_2 because the first product of their photosynthetic reactions, a four-carbon sugar, is used to produce three-carbon sugars and CO_2. The carbon dioxide is then used in the Calvin cycle in nearby cells.

A CHAMPION PHOTOSYNTHESIZER

Nearly one fourth of all the food calories eaten by people and farm animals can be traced to the energy captured from the sun by corn (maize) plants. Corn is the largest crop in the United States. Each year American farmers plant 70 million acres (28 million hectares) of corn plants—enough to cover the entire state of Arizona. Corn also has another distinction: this C_4 plant is the best photosynthesizer of all the world's major grain crops.

Corn has been around for quite some time. Central American Indians began growing it about 7,000 years ago. By the time Columbus came to the New World, Native Americans had developed more than 200 kinds of corn and were growing it from Chile to Canada.

CAM plants have evolved another variation of photosynthesis to adapt to hot, dry climates. Pineapples, many cacti, and most succulent plants (such as ice plants and jade plants) are CAM plants. They are similar to C_4 plants. They open their stomates only at night and fix CO_2 into a four-carbon compound, which is

A variety of cacti grow in deserts. They use a particular type of photosynthesis to adapt to the hot, dry climate.

stored at night and used by the Calvin cycle during the day. CAM stands for *c*rassulacean *a*cid *m*etabolism, because it was first discovered in the plant family Crassulaceae (jade plants).

In C_4 plants the C_4 pathway and the Calvin cycle occur in different cells. But in CAM plants, the two cycles occur within the same cell—just at different times. The C_4 pathway takes place at night, and the Calvin cycle occurs during the day.

FOUR

PHOTOSYNTHESIS TODAY

Living things are joined together in our world by a natural balance. All of life is linked in a double chain. One chain is made up of energy, and the other chain is the materials of life. Energy flows through life in a one-way stream. Energy comes from the sun, passes through living things, and eventually leaves our planet as heat, spreading out into space. But the molecules of life—water, oxygen, carbon dioxide, and sugar—circulate in an endless recycled loop.

✦ THE ENERGY HIGHWAY ✦

Green plants and other photosynthetic organisms capture energy from sunlight and put it into the chemical bonds of sugar through the process of photosynthesis. Sugar is the universal food and energy source of most living things. Herbivores get sugar from plants, carnivores get it from eating plant eaters, and decomposers get it by breaking down the waste products and dead bodies of the other living creatures.

The food chain is an upside-down pyramid. Most of the energy that a living creature takes in is not stored in its body. Most gets used up in **metabolism**—the chemical processes that go on inside an organism to build up and break down materials. So, it takes a lot more energy to make "food" than we get when we eat that food. The higher up a food is on the food pyramid, the more energy it took to make that food. Cattle, which are midway up on the food pyramid, eat more than 10 pounds (about 5 kg) of grain, or a far larger amount of grass, to produce just 1 pound (about 0.5 kg) of beef. So, it is a much more efficient use of energy to eat from the bottom of the food pyramid than closer to the top. It has been estimated that if Americans cut down the amount of meat they eat by just 10 percent, 100 million people could be fed with crops grown on the land freed from growing livestock feed.

✦ THE RECYCLING OF MATTER ✦

In addition to energy, living things need materials to build their bodies. All of the materials that make up living things are part of a circular flow between living creatures. Organisms take in materials from their environment in order to grow and repair body tissues. These materials are returned to the environment through waste products, or when the organism dies. Then they are used by other living things.

When a cow eats grass, the waste products are returned to the soil. The matter that was in the original grass may pass through bacteria, earthworms, grass again, and then may even be eaten by the same cow.

Unlike other animals, humans take materials from the environment and make them into things that other living things can't use for a very long time. Eventually everything breaks down, but many man-made materials, such as plastics, take far longer than most other materials to be turned back into usable forms.

THREE WAYS PHOTOSYNTHESIS KEEPS OUR WORLD ALIVE

Photosynthesis helps in three ways to keep humans and other animals alive:
1. It provides the fuel from which we get energy.
2. It provides the oxygen to burn the fuel.
3. It keeps the earth's climate in balance.

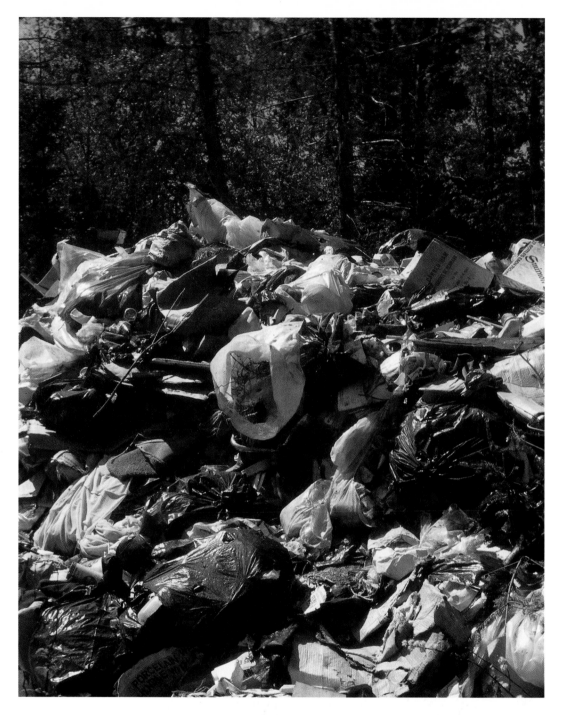

Plastics do not readily break down. Some plastics can be recycled, and scientists have developed others that are biodegradable, but plastic is still a huge waste problem.

✦ OXYGEN–CARBON DIOXIDE BALANCE ✦

Animals breathe out carbon dioxide as a waste product during respiration when they burn food to produce energy. Plants use that carbon dioxide to make sugar during photosynthesis, and produce oxygen as a waste product. In the big picture of the **ecosystem**, this give-and-take forms a circular flow of materials in a perfect balance.

Plants provide a constant supply of oxygen and use up the carbon dioxide waste products that animals produce to get energy from food. Without photosynthesis, all of the oxygen in our atmosphere would be used up, and there would be much too much carbon dioxide. The balance between plant photosynthesis and animal respiration keeps the right proportions of oxygen and carbon dioxide in our atmosphere. There is enough oxygen for animals to get energy from food, and enough carbon dioxide in the air for plants to make food using the energy from the sun.

✦ THE OXYGEN CYCLE ✦

Oxygen makes up 21 percent of the volume of our atmosphere. But most of the oxygen on our planet is combined with other elements, such as in water (H_2O), or in rocks, where it is combined with minerals such as silicon, aluminum, iron, calcium, and magnesium. Silicon dioxide is the most common compound in the earth's crust. (This is the basic material of sand.)

Sand is formed when rocks weather. This tiny grain, greatly magnified, is composed mainly of silicon dioxide (quartz).

Oxygen is constantly being removed from the atmosphere in the process of "weathering," during which the oxygen combines with mineral compounds. About 5 percent of the earth's crust is iron, for example. Almost all iron is combined with oxygen, but half is in a form that could hold more oxygen (ferrous iron). When it is exposed to air it reacts with oxygen (becomes oxidized), and oxygen is removed from the atmosphere. Scientists believe that this process has locked up an amount of oxygen in the rocks of the earth equal to 70 percent of the oxygen in the atmosphere today!

Animals and plants use up oxygen through respiration. It is also used up in the burning of fuels such as oil, gas, and coal. *Photosynthesis by green plants and algae makes up the only major source of oxygen that replaces the supply.*

Tropical rain forests cover only 3 percent of the earth's surface, but scientists estimate they are responsible for 20 percent of the photosynthesis that occurs on our planet. That's why environmentalists have called them the "lungs" of the planet. However, most experts say that rain forests make very little overall contribution to the amount of oxygen that is added to our atmosphere. Why? Plants undergo cellular respiration just like animals, so they take in oxygen and release carbon dioxide into the atmosphere. Moreover, their fruits are eaten by animals, and the CO_2 that was removed from the atmosphere is returned as the animals use the stored food energy. The same happens when the trees die.

Observing Carbon Dioxide

Carbon dioxide is an invisible and odorless gas. Limewater (a solution of calcium carbonate—chalk—in water) can be used to test for it.

Put 20 milliliters of limewater into a small jar or beaker. Blow into the jar with a straw. The limewater will turn a milky color because there is carbon dioxide in your breath when you exhale.

Now put 20 milliliters of limewater into a small beaker and place a candle next to it. Light the candle, and then place a gallon jar over the candle and beaker. The candle burns up all the oxygen and produces carbon dioxide. Will the limewater turn cloudy if you don't light a candle under the jar?

This rain forest in Costa Rica is being destroyed by clear cutting to turn the land into farming areas.

✦ THE CARBON CYCLE ✦

Living plants absorb carbon dioxide and use it to form leaves, stem, and fruit. Carbon dioxide dissolved in water is used by water plants as they grow.

Animals on land and in the ocean eat plants and use the carbon to form shells, skin, bone, and muscle. Animals exhale carbon dioxide when food is broken down. When animals die, the carbon in their bodies is eventually oxidized to carbon dioxide and returned to the atmosphere, except for the carbon that becomes trapped in minerals in the earth's crust.

There are large amounts of carbon locked in rocks and solid materials in the earth. Skeletons of the shells of animals that lived in the oceans millions of years ago can be found in rocks. In England the white cliffs of Dover are made up of the tiny skeletons of sea animals that lived long ago. Coral reefs and some entire islands in the Pacific Ocean are made up of coral skeletons.

Coal, which people dig up out of the ground, and oil, which they pump out of underground deposits, were formed millions of years ago from plants and animals that had died. Scientists believe there is forty times as much carbon in coal and oil deposits as there is in all the plants and animals now alive.

✦ THE GREENHOUSE EFFECT ✦

As the human population grows around the world, people are burning more and more fuels—coal, gas, oil, and wood—to heat homes and businesses and run cars and trucks. Like respiration, burning fuel releases carbon dioxide. Meanwhile, each year people cut down forests to clear land for growing crops and raising animals, for firewood and lumber, and to build houses and factories. The forests of the world produce enormous amounts of oxygen and take in huge amounts of carbon dioxide. Many scientists worry about the disappearing forests. They fear that the amount of carbon dioxide in the atmosphere is increasing at an alarming rate.

Carbon dioxide and other gases in the atmosphere act as an insulating blanket to keep heat from escaping. Without these gases to trap heat, the earth would be too cold for us to live. The heat-trapping effect of the atmospheric gases is similar to what happens in a greenhouse, where the glass windows and roof hold in heat from sunlight. So the effects of carbon dioxide on our planet are often referred to as the **greenhouse effect**.

Although a certain amount of warming has been good for life on earth, too much carbon dioxide would trap too much heat. If the world warmed up much higher than our present-day temperatures, the ice caps at the North and

South Pole would melt. When glaciers melt, the water released causes the sea to rise. Over the last 100 years the greenhouse effect has caused the sea level around the world to rise 4 inches (10 cm). This might not seem like a lot, but many cities are at sea level, and beaches all around the world are shrinking as the sea level rises. Scientists worry that if this continues, cities on the coasts around the world may be flooded.

A furious argument has been raging about whether we should protect our few remaining old-growth forests (such as the giant sequoias in California) or harvest the trees for lumber. Both sides are using the greenhouse effect to support their position. Those who believe we should protect old-growth forests argue that these huge photosynthesizing trees remove large amounts of carbon dioxide from the atmosphere. But those who want to continue harvesting these ancient trees say that if we replace the old trees with new seedlings, more photosynthesis will occur and more CO_2 will be removed.

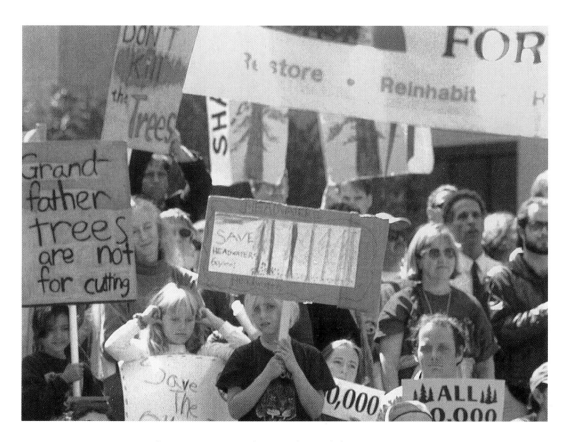

This is just one of a number of demonstrations carried out to save our old-growth forests.

Young trees do photosynthesize much more, relative to their size and weight, because they grow rapidly. However, only half of a harvested tree is used for lumber. The roots and most of the branches are left behind to decompose. In addition, most of the wood that is harvested is turned into products such as paper, sawdust, and fuel, which are burned or decompose in only a few years. This means that the carbon that was in the tree is put back into the atmosphere as CO_2!

TROUBLE IN GRASSLAND

Scientists had hoped that acid rain, which contains nitrogen compounds and other substances that stimulate plant growth, would help to soak up the extra carbon dioxide that our industrial world is producing. But ecologists who studied plots in a Minnesota prairie recently discovered that this "solution" may not work.

The native grasses in North America are mainly C_4 plants, which not only thrive in hot weather but can get along with very limited amounts of nitrogen. When European settlers came to America, they brought with them various plants and seeds, which turned into weeds in their new home. The imported weeds are mainly C_3 plants, which are real nitrogen hogs.

When the researchers added nitrogen to the prairie grasslands, the C_3 weeds overran the plots, choking out the native C_4 grasses. The weeds stored a lot of nitrogen, and when they died, they sparked a growth spurt among the soil microbes that break down plant matter. The multiplying microbes allowed the nitrogen that was stored in the weeds to run off and pollute the water, while the plants' carbon was released into the air. As a result, the weeds stored less than half as much carbon as the native grasses, which decompose more slowly.

✦ HUMANS USE PRODUCTS OF PHOTOSYNTHESIS ✦

Many of the basic materials that people use are directly or indirectly dependent on photosynthesis. Textile fibers, lumber, pulp products, vegetable fats, gums, and resins all exist because of photosynthesis. Coal was formed from plants. Natural gas and petroleum were formed by chemical changes in the remains of plants and animals that fed on plants.

✦ STORED FOOD ✦

Usually plants produce more sugar than they can use right away. Some of the sugar may be turned into starch for storage. Food is stored by plants to use when growing conditions are more difficult. It is also stored to provide energy and growing materials for the next generation of plants.

Sugar and starch can be stored in the plant's flowers, fruits, seeds, roots, and stem. These are the parts of the plant that animals and people usually eat for food.

WHERE'S THE FOOD?

Cereal plants and legumes store food in seeds. Carrots, beets, and turnips store food in their roots. Potatoes store food in tubers, which are actually swollen stems even though they form underground. Bananas store sugar and starch in fruits. Artichokes store food in their flowers.

✦ CARBOHYDRATES ✦

Glucose, also called dextrose, is a simple sugar. It is the main product of photosynthesis. Another simple six-carbon plant sugar is fructose ("fruit sugar"). Some plants join a glucose and a fructose unit together to form **sucrose**—the sugar we use to sweeten foods and drinks.

Other important carbohydrates that are made by plants include starch and cellulose. Cellulose is not a food for plants but a building material. Other carbohydrates produced are forms of stored food. In some plants, such as sugar beet, sugarcane, and onion, sucrose is stored as food. But in most plants, starch is the main storage product.

Glucose is transported from the leaf, where it is produced, to other parts of the plant. But when the sun is shining, glucose may be produced in the leaf faster than it is used or transported. This extra glucose may be changed into starch as a temporary storage product in the chloroplasts. Later this starch will be reconverted to sugar and transported from the leaf to other parts of the plant.

At night more glucose is transported from the leaf. The leaves lose weight during the night as the starch is converted to sugar and removed.

✦ PROTEINS ✦

Like carbohydrates, proteins contain the elements carbon, hydrogen, and oxygen, but they also contain nitrogen (and sometimes sulfur) as well. Proteins are stored in seeds, especially those of legumes, corms, bulbs, rhizomes, buds, and storage roots. Large quantities of proteins are needed during growth. When a seed sprouts, stored protein is converted into soluble forms and is transported to the growing seedling.

A Starch Test for Photosynthesis

A test for starch can be used to see whether photosynthesis is occurring in a leaf because glucose is quickly turned into starch as a temporary storage form when a lot of glucose is being produced. If a leaf is kept in the dark for several hours and the chlorophyll is removed by soaking the leaf in alcohol, staining it with iodine (which tests for starch) will not show much starch present (the leaf will stain brown). But a leaf that has been absorbing sunlight all day will stain blue or black when tested the same way. This shows that starch is present.

Soybeans, like other legumes, store food in the seeds. Soybeans are particularly rich in oil.

Amino acids, the building blocks of proteins, are needed by plants and animals. Green plants can produce all of the amino acids they need. Animals can form some amino acids from the food in their diet, but most must be obtained from plants. Essential amino acids are ones that animals cannot form themselves, and nonessential amino acids are ones that animals can transform from other amino acids.

✦ FATS AND OILS ✦

Fats and oils are formed from sugars, too. They contain the same chemical elements as sugar, but the ratio of oxygen atoms to carbon atoms is much higher in sugars. Oils are also an important storage source for energy. They are stored mainly in seeds and also in fruits. Seeds rich in oil include Brazil nut, castor bean, coconut, corn, cotton, nutmeg, peanut, palm, soybean, sunflower, and tung. Fruits high in oil include avocado and olives. Fifty percent of the dry weight of olives is oil! Seeds may contain oil as the only stored food, or they may contain both starch and oil. In animals, fats are the main form of food storage. Animals can form many fatty materials from carbohydrates.

WHAT'S THE DIFFERENCE BETWEEN FATS AND OILS?

Chemically, fats and oils belong to the same family. But at room temperature, fats are normally solid and oils are liquid.

FIVE

Photosynthesis in the Future

Scientists today are actively studying photosynthesis. They believe that this process holds the important keys to our future. Photosynthesis is tied to almost all human needs. Plants supply all of our food, either directly or indirectly through plant-eating animals. Photosynthesis is also responsible for most of our energy sources—the energy that is stored in coal, oil, gas, and firewood all came from the sun by way of photosynthesis. Photosynthesis also fills many of our needs for fibers and building materials.

If we can learn to understand and control the photosynthetic process, we can learn how to more efficiently use our land, and to increase the amount of food, fiber, fuel, and wood.

Once we can effectively reproduce the photosynthetic process we can develop ways to more efficiently use solar energy as a major energy source. Scientists are also using things they have learned about photosynthesis to design supercomputers and medical treatments.

✦ PLANT FOODS FOR THE FUTURE ✦

As the human population continues to grow, more food will be needed, but there will be less space available to grow that food. Farmers and scientists have already greatly improved the efficiency of growing plant crops for food. Better fertilizers, insect control, and specially bred plants have greatly increased the amount of food that can be grown in smaller areas, as well as improved the nutritional value of many foods.

Scientists have also developed even more-efficient ways to grow food. Hydroponics is growing food in water. Scientists can add to the water the exact proportion of minerals that will produce the best growing conditions for a particular kind of plant. Dr. William Gericke, a professor at the University of California, coined the term **hydroponics**. In 1930, using hydroponics, he grew a 25-foot (8-meter) tomato plant!

The root system of plants being grown by the hydroponic method. In this method, plants develop in water and without soil.

✦ SUPER FOOD PRODUCERS ✦

Most plants are limited in the amount of food that they can produce. Much of the energy that plants use from the sun is not used to produce food. Plants must produce roots, flowers, fruits, wood, and other structures that do not contain chlorophyll. The most efficient food-producing plant would be one in which all its parts contain chlorophyll. That way, the whole plant would be designed to use the sun's energy to produce food.

Most algae are microscopic single-cell plantlike creatures. Algae are super-efficient photosynthesizers—they can produce a much greater amount of food from the energy they get from the sun. (Another plus is that most grow in bodies of water, and so do not take up any land space.) In Asia and other parts of the world, people eat seaweed, which is a form of algae. Food scientists are working on various ways to produce good-tasting foods from algae. Artificial flavors and aromas and techniques to give "**single-cell protein**" a texture similar to meat or other common foods are helping in the effort to use this cheap and plentiful source to keep up with the world's growing needs for food.

✦ FOOD FOR SPACE ✦

If space travel ever gets off the ground, algae could also play a major role. On a long trip, such as a journey from Earth to Mars, it would be difficult to store large amounts of food and oxygen. Algae could provide a source for both of these needs. Specially bred or "genetically engineered" algae growing in tanks aboard the spacecraft could supply the astronauts with a continuous supply of food. They would also help to maintain the supply of oxygen on board and use up the carbon dioxide that the astronauts breathed out.

✦ DESIGNING BETTER PLANTS ✦

Many plants undergo a process called photorespiration. It wastes a lot of the plant's photosynthetic efficiency. Photosynthesis researchers are trying to understand exactly what the function of photorespiration is. When scientists can better understand a process like this, they can change it to design better plants. Researchers hope to produce new crops that will make much better use of the sunlight they absorb.

C_4 plants do not undergo photorespiration. Using genetic engineering, scientists hope to be able to breed some of the features of C_4 photosynthesis into important food-producing C_3 plants. Soybeans, for example are a great source of

*Algae such as this forming a scum on a lake
could one day be a source of food for astronauts
on long journeys in space.*

protein, but they are limited in the amount of crops they can produce. If soybeans underwent C_4 photosynthesis, scientists could greatly increase the amount of these highly nutritious crops produced in the same space of land.

✦ PHOTOSYNTHETIC PRODUCTS AND ENERGY ✦

Ethanol, or grain alcohol, is made by fermenting sugars and starches. In some places, such as Brazil, it is a major automobile fuel. In some parts of the United States, ethanol is added to gasoline to help reduce the amount of harmful pollutants that are put into the atmosphere with normal gasoline. Ethanol is also easily converted to ethylene, which is used in the petrochemical industry. Scientists hope to be able someday to use cellulose as a cheap source of ethanol. Cellulose is the major component of wood and other plant materials. Some microorganisms are able to convert cellulose to sugar and then to ethanol.

Scientists are also exploring ways to use photosynthesis directly as an energy source. The overall process of photosynthesis is not very efficient, but the first steps in the process, in which sunlight is converted into chemical energy, are very efficient. Researchers are trying to build artificial devices that work like plants to capture and harvest solar energy. Scientists have already successfully developed artificial photosynthetic reaction centers that are nearly as good at storing solar energy as chemical or electrical energy as those found in plants. In the future, researchers hope to develop even more-efficient solar energy harvesting devices based on the natural process in plants.

Solar panels can collect the sun's energy for various uses, often to provide electric current. A similar system may provide energy for artificial photosynthesis.

When we burn petroleum fuels, other by-products such as hydrocarbons and nitrogen oxides are released into the atmosphere in addition to carbon dioxide. These pollutants are not produced with the artificial photosynthetic reaction centers. Perhaps someday this technology, which is based on the natural process of photosynthesis, will provide us with a clean energy source.

✦ PHOTOSYNTHESIS AND SAFER PESTICIDES ✦

Several major herbicides work by interfering with the photosynthetic process in plants. By understanding photosynthesis better, researchers hope to be able to design safer, more effective, more selective **herbicides** to control weeds.

CAREER WATCH: PHOTOSYNTHESIS

Farming: Breeding and growing new, more efficient crops; studying and applying the best conditions for growth; growing single-cell protein in the sea and in factory vats; food science studies to improve taste and nutrition.

*"**Pharming**"*: Genetic engineering to transfer genes from one species to another—even animal genes to plant cells—to mass-produce valuable biological products cheaply.

✦ PHOTOSYNTHETIC COMPUTERS? ✦

Computers have changed and have become a part of our everyday lives. Scientists are exploring the idea of using photosynthetic principles to develop smaller, more efficient computers. Scientists are hoping that learning how plants absorb light, and how they control the way energy is moved to reaction centers and converted to electrical and chemical energy will help them design computers that work on a tiny scale—where each part is only a few molecules big. Researchers have already made some progress in this direction.

✦ PHOTOSYNTHESIS AND MEDICINE ✦

Light has a lot of energy. Sometimes this energy can cause damage to living organisms. Light energy causes aging of the skin and skin cancer in humans and other animals. Plants have developed protective mechanisms that limit the

Corn is a major crop and has many uses worldwide.
Each of the many chloroplasts in a corn plant (inset) contains
chlorophyll and is the site of photosynthesis. Our understanding
of the process can help to increase crop production.

amount of damage light can cause. Scientists are studying how light energy causes tissue damage and are trying to learn from plants ways to prevent light damage from occurring in humans.

Scientists are also using substances related to chlorophyll to fight cancer. These substances will collect in cancerous tumor tissue. When light is shined on the tumors, the cancer cells are killed because of photochemical damage, while the surrounding tissue remains unharmed. In other experiments, the chlorophyll-like substances act as a dye to show doctors the border between cancerous and healthy tissue.

GLOSSARY

antenna pigments—chlorophyll and other pigment molecules in a photosystem that gather light energy.

ATP—adenosine triphosphate: a chemical compound used by living organisms for the temporary storage of energy.

bacteriochlorophyll—a form of chlorophyll produced by purple bacteria.

C_3 plant—a plant in which the first stable product of photosynthesis (via the Calvin cycle) is a sugar containing three carbon atoms per molecule. Examples include wheat, rice, oats, and soybeans.

C_4 plant—a plant in which the first stable product of photosynthesis is a sugar containing four carbon atoms per molecule. Examples include corn, sugarcane, and crabgrass.

Calvin cycle—the dark reactions of photosynthesis, in which simple sugars are formed from carbon dioxide.

CAM plants—plants adapted to hot, dry conditions that open their stomates only at night and produce a four-carbon sugar as the first stable product of photosynthesis. Examples include pineapples, cacti, and jade plants.

carbohydrates—a family of chemical compounds containing carbon, hydrogen, and oxygen; they include sugars and starches.

carbon dioxide—a gas found in the atmosphere; its molecules each contain one atom of carbon and two atoms of oxygen.

carnivores—animals that eat other animals.

carotenoids—red, orange, and yellow pigments that help in photosynthesis.

catalyst—a chemical that helps chemical reactions to take place but itself remains unchanged.

cellulose—a fibrous substance in plant cells that humans cannot digest.

chemosynthesis—food production by living organisms using energy stored in chemical compounds.

chlorobium chlorophyll—a form of chlorophyll produced by green sulfur bacteria.

chlorophyll—a green pigment in plants and certain bacteria that absorbs sunlight energy.

chloroplasts—structures in plant cells that contain chlorophyll; the site of photosynthesis.

consumers—organisms that eat other organisms in the community.

dark reactions of photosynthesis—the chemical reactions of photosynthesis that do not require light energy; in these reactions, energy stored in ATP is used to build simple sugars from carbon dioxide; also called the Calvin cycle.

decomposers—organisms that break down wastes and dead matter, returning their components to the environment.

ecosystem—a biological community, in which organisms live and interact with each other and their environment.

electron transport chain—a series of chlorophyll and enzyme molecules that transfer electrons in the photosynthetic reactions producing ATP.

electron—a tiny particle with a negative electric charge; normally found on the outer part of an atom, electrons can be transferred from one atom to another. Moving electrons produce an electric current.

enzyme—a catalyst (usually a protein) that helps chemical reactions to take place in living organisms.

food web—the interconnected food chains in an ecosystem.

food chain—a sequence of organisms, each of which is eaten by the next member in the chain.

glucose—a simple sugar containing six carbon atoms, twelve hydrogen atoms, and six oxygen atoms per molecule.

greenhouse effect—a general warming believed to be occuring because of the heat-trapping effect of carbon dioxide and other gases in the atmosphere.

herbicide—a chemical used to kill off undesirable plants (weeds).

herbivores—animals that eat mainly plants.

hydroponics—a technique of growing food plants in water, to which mineral nutrients are added.

light reactions of photosynthesis—the chemical reactions of photosynthesis that take place only in the light; in these reactions sunlight energy is used to form ATP.

metabolism—the chemical process that goes on inside an organism to build up and break down materials.

mitochondria—structures inside a cell in which respiration takes place; sugars are broken down, forming ATP.

molecule—the smallest unit of a chemical compound that still has all the characteristics of that compound.

NADP—nicotinamide adenine dinucleotide phosphate; a compound that accepts electrons and hydrogen ions in the light reactions of photosynthesis, forming NADPH.

omnivores—animals that eat both plants and animals.

organelles—structures inside a cell that perform a specific function, such as chloroplasts (photosynthesis) and mitochondria (respiration).

3-PGA—3-phosphoglycerate, the first three-carbon compound formed in the Calvin cycle.

"pharming"—the use of genetic engineering techniques to mass-produce valuable biological products cheaply in plants. The name comes from "pharmaceutical" (drug) and "farming."

phloem—fibrous tubes that carry food from leaves to other parts of the plant.

photochemical reactions—reactions in which light energy is used to form chemical bonds.

photon—a traveling particle of light; a light unit; a packet of light energy.

photorespiration—a water-conserving process used by C_3 plants, which uses oxygen and produces carbon dioxide but does not form sugars.

photosynthesis—a process in which living organisms use sunlight energy to make carbohydrates from carbon dioxide and water, producing oxygen as a by-product.

photosystem—groups of 250 to 400 chlorophyll molecules that work together to gather sunlight energy and store some of it in chemical form, in ATP.

phycobilins—red and blue pigments that help in photosynthesis.

producers—organisms that make their own food and provide food for other organisms in the ecosystem.

purple sulfur bacteria—bacteria that produce carbohydrates by photosynthesis but do not release oxygen.

reaction center—the single chlorophyll molecule in a photosystem that can use light energy for photochemical reactions.

respiration—a process in living cells in which carbohydrates and other organic carbon compounds are reacted with oxygen, releasing energy and producing carbon dioxide as a waste product.

rubisco—the enzyme involved in joining carbon dioxide (CO_2) and the five-carbon sugar RuBP to form a six-carbon sugar in the first step of the Calvin cycle.

RuBP—ribulose-5-biphosphate, a five-carbon sugar formed in the Calvin cycle.

single-cell protein—protein-rich food produced from algae and processed to give it an appealing texture, appearance, taste, and odor.

starches—carbohydrates made up of large numbers of sugar units linked together.

stomates—openings on the undersides of leaves through which gases can pass to and out of the leaves; they can be closed off by guard cells.

stroma—the inner chamber of a chloroplast.

sucrose—table sugar; its molecule consists of one molecule of glucose and one of fructose (another simple sugar), chemically joined together.

thylakoids—stacks of disklike membrane sacs inside the stroma of a chloroplast; chlorophyll is found in the thylakoid membranes.

xylem—fibrous tubes through which water and minerals are transported from plant roots to the leaves.

For Further Information

BOOKS

Asimov, Issac. *How Did We Find Out About Photosynthesis?* New York: Walker, 1989.

Burnie, David. *Plant and Flower.* New York: Knopf, 1989.

Dow, Leslie. *Incredible Plants.* Alexandria, VA: Time Life, 1997.

Massa, Renato, Monica Carabella, and Lorenzo Fornasari. *The Breathing Earth.* Austin, TX: Steck-Vaughn, 1997.

Ross, Bill. *Straight From the Bear's Mouth.* New York: Simon & Schuster, 1995.

Silverstein, A., Virginia, and Robert. *Plants.* New York: Twenty-First Century Books, 1996.

Taylor, Barbara. *Incredible Plants.* New York: DK Publishing, 1997.

INTERNET RESOURCES

http://arc-genl.life.uiuc.edu/Bioph354/lect20.html "Lecture 20. Introduction to Photosynthesis." (University of Illinois at Champlain-Urbana, with lecture notes, color illustrations, review articles, research reports, interactive tutorials to download, and links)

http://boe.cabe.k12.wv.us/cmhs/lab4.html "AP Biology Lab 4: Plant Pigments & Photosynthesis." (High school lab experiment)

http://esg-www.mit.edu.8001/esgbio/ps/psdir.html "7.01 Hypertextbook: Photosynthesis." (Chapter on photosynthesis with color illustrations; Massachusetts Institute of Technology)

http://photoscience.la.asu.edu/photosyn/default.html "ASU Photosynthesis Center." (Activities at the Arizona State University center, articles on photosynthesis, and links to other excellent web sites)

http://plantcell.lu.se/ "Plant Cell Biology." (Lund University, Sweden, articles on photosynthesis and research activities, including animated illustrations)

http://seawifs.gsfc.nasa.gov/SEAWIFS/LIVING_OCEAN/TEACHER1.html "The Living Ocean: The Role of the Oceans in Carbon Exchange." (NASA satellite surveys revealing distribution of phytoplankton, carbon cycle)

http://www.emc.maricopa.edu/bio/bio181/BIOBK/BioBookPS.html# Table of Contents "Photosynthesis." (Text by M. J. Farabee with vivid illustrations from various sources; not as dense and technical as MIT Hypertextbook and UICU review articles)

http://www.ktca.org/newtons/9/phytosy.html "Photosynthesis: How do plants make food?" (Newton's Apple Teacher's Guide with activity pages)

INDEX

acid rain, 42

ADP (adenosine diphosphate), 17

algae, 24, 48, 49

amino acids, 27, 45

antenna pigments, 23–24

Archaebacteria, 8

Aristotle, 12

ATP (adenosine triphosphate), 17, 25, 26, 28–30

bacteriochlorophyll, 24

begonias, 7

biomass, 9

Blackman, F.F., 17

blue-green bacteria, 23

brown algae, 24

C_3 plants, 31, 42

C_4 plants, 31–32, 42, 48–49

Calvin, Melvin, 17–18, 30, 31

Calvin cycle, 18, 30, 32, 33

CAM (crassulacean acid metabolism) plants, 32–33

cancer, 53

carbohydrates, 13, 15, 16, 30, 43, 45

carbon dioxide, 5, 8, 13, 15–17, 21, 25–28, 32, 37, 38, 40, 42

carnivores, 9, 34

carotenoids, 23, 25

catalyst, chlorophyll as, 6

Caventou, Joseph Bienaime, 16

cellulose, 6, 26–27, 43, 49

chemosynthesis, 8

chlorobium chlorophyll, 24

chlorophyll, 6, 7, 16, 22–24, 27, 48, 52

chloroplasts, 16, 22–23, 25, 28–31, 43, 52

coal, 40, 42

computers, 51

consumers, 9–10

corn (maize), 32, 52

crabgrass, 32

cyanobacteria, 25

dark reactions of photosynthesis, 17, 18, 25

decomposers, 11, 34

diatoms, 24
dinosaurs, 27
DNA, 27

ecosystem, 37
electromagnetic radiation, 7
electron, 23, 25, 28
electron transport chain, 25
enzymes, 17, 25
ethanol (grain alcohol), 49
ethylene, 49

fats, 6, 45
ferrous iron, 38
food chain, 8–9, 34
food web, 8
fructose, 43

genetic engineering, 48, 51
Gericke, William, 47
glucose (dextrose), 17, 26–27, 30, 43
grana, 22
greenhouse effect, 40–41

Helmont, Jan Baptista van, 12–13
herbicides, 51
herbivores, 9, 34
hydrocarbons, 51
hydrogen, 15, 17, 25, 26, 28
hydroponics, 47

infrared light, 7
Ingenhousz, Jan, 13

leaves, 6, 20
light, 5–7, 16, 17, 51, 53
light reactions of photosynthesis, 17, 18, 25
lithotrophs, 8

Mayer, Julius, 15
metabolism, 34–35
mitochondria, 28–29
molecule, 6

NADP (nicotinamide adenine dinucleotide phosphate), 25, 26, 30
natural gas, 42
Niel, C.B. van, 16
nitrogen, 16, 42, 44
nitrogen oxides, 51

oil, 40, 42
oils, 45
old-growth forests, 41
omnivores, 10
organelles, 22, 28, 29
oxygen, 5–6, 13, 16, 17, 25, 26, 28, 32, 35, 37–38

3-PGA, 30
Pelletier, Pierre Joseph, 16
"pharming," 51
phloem, 19
photochemmical reactions, 23
photon, 7, 23, 25
photorespiration, 32, 48
photosynthesis, defined, 5
photosystem, 23
phycobilins, 23, 25
pigments, 23–25
plastics, 35, 36
Priestley, Joseph, 13, 14
producers, 9
proteins, 6, 44–45
purple sulfur bacteria, 16

rain forests, 38, 39
reaction center, 23, 24

red algae, 25
respiration, 28, 29, 37, 38
RNA, 27
rocks, 37, 40
roots, 19, 20
rubisco, 30
RuBP, 30

Sachs, Julius von, 16
sand, 37
Saussure, Nicholas Theodore de, 15
silicon dioxide, 37
Silurian period, 8
single-cell protein, 48, 51
soil, 12–13
solar energy, 5–7, 50
soybeans, 44, 48–49
starches, 6, 13, 15, 43, 44

stems, 6, 19
stomates, 21
stroma, 22, 25
sucrose, 43
sugar, 6, 9, 13, 15, 22, 25–26, 29–30, 34, 43
sulfur bacteria, 28

thylakoids, 22, 23, 25
tubeworms, 8

ultraviolet light, 7

water, 5, 16, 17, 28, 47
weathering, 38
Willstatter, Richard, 16
Woodward, Robert Burns, 16

xylem, 19, 20